In three short books, Pastor Joe Thorn offers a helpful treatment on the local church that is biblical, baptistic, and Calvinistic—and simultaneously fresh and practical. This is ideal for those who desire a better understanding of what the church is designed to be and do as a community of faith seeking to follow Jesus into the world with the gospel.

In *The Heart of the Church*, Thorn walks the reader through the gospel and related doctrines, demonstrating how what we believe forms who we are as God's people. In *The Character of the Church*, the essential components of a church are laid out in a clear and practical way showing what is needed for overall church he... *Life of the Church*, Thorn offers a fresh pe... how the church can live on mission ... and the good of others in tang...

ED STETZER
Billy Graham Distinguished Cha...

I'd like to pass out *The Character of the Church* to every one of our church members. It's that good! It's a simple yet profound primer on the nature of the church. It gives a brief overview on the authority of the Bible, the ordinances, matters of church membership, and church discipline. These are essential for all believers to know and understand.

DAVE FURMAN
Pastor, Redeemer Church of Dubai, and author of *Being There: How to Love Those Who Are Hurting*

The Life of the Church is a helpful treatise on worship that will edify the church. Joe is careful to ensure his exhortations spring from Scripture itself, which makes this book applicable for Christians everywhere. It was a joy to read about the many aspects of the life that Christ has purchased for us with His own blood.

GLORIA FURMAN
Cross-cultural worker and author of *Missional Motherhood* and *Alive in Him*

The Heart of the Church is a brief and accessible theology of the gospel. It is simple, but not simplistic. It offers profound truths in everyday language. This book will help new Christians and serve as an encouraging reminder to mature ones.

RICHARD C. BARCELLOS
Pastor, Grace Reformed Baptist Church in Palmdale, CA, and author of *The Lord's Supper as a Means of Grace*

THE
life
OF THE
CHURCH

—

THE TABLE, PULPIT, AND SQUARE

—

JOE THORN

MOODY PUBLISHERS
CHICAGO

Edited by Kevin P. Emmert
Cover and interior design: Erik M. Peterson
Author photo: Anthony Benedetto

All websites listed herein are accurate at the time of publication but may change in the future or cease to exist. The listing of website references and resources does not imply publisher endorsement of the site's entire contents. Groups and organizations are listed for informational purposes, and listing does not imply publisher endorsement of their activities.

ISBN: 978-0-8024-1469-4

We hope you enjoy this book from Moody Publishers. Our goal is to provide high-quality, thought-provoking books and products that connect truth to your real needs and challenges. For more information on other books and products written and produced from a biblical perspective, go to www.moodypublishers.com or write to:

Moody Publishers
820 N. LaSalle Boulevard
Chicago, IL 60610

1 3 5 7 9 10 8 6 4 2

Printed in the United States of America

To the members of Redeemer Fellowship,
who have demonstrated love, faith, sacrifice,
and service in the life of our church.

contents

INTRODUCTION

𝒜 church is not what most people think it is. As I explained in *The Character of the Church*, the Greek word in the New Testament from which we derive the word "church" is *ekklesia*, meaning "assembly." That term can be used to describe any kind of assembly. But when applied to a local church, it denotes something unique. A local church is an assembly of believers in Jesus who are united together by a common confession, are gathered in one localized body, are ruled by Scripture, and work together for the mission given to them by their Lord.

But even with a clear definition of a church, more must be said. How will a church live? What must it do? For a united group of Christians to be a healthy church like that modeled in the New Testament, it must possess five essential characteristics: (1) Scripture must be rightly preached; (2) the ordinances must be rightly administered; (3) leadership must be formed by and function in accordance with Scripture;

(4) discipline must be carried out with grace; and (5) the mission of the church must be shared and embraced by all. But what is the main work of the church, and how should a congregation go about carrying out those responsibilities?

The church can do many things, but there is one primary responsibility given to the church by our Lord: to make disciples (Matt. 28:18–20). Many churches seek to do the work entrusted to them by Jesus through the careful implementation of programs and teaching supported by well-developed systems for assimilation. Others opt for a more "organic" approach to disciple-making, offering less structure and cultivating a more relationship-based culture. Some churches view discipleship as primarily, if not exclusively, a matter of instruction and indoctrination, and thus neglect the need for relationships and working together. Other churches neglect doctrine while offering ministry services aimed only at practical matters.

In order to rightly understand how the church goes about making disciples, I believe it is helpful to start with the big picture, move to the level of principle, and then establish practices and rhythms that are easily translatable to other contexts.

WHAT IS A DISCIPLE?

Throughout His entire earthly ministry, Jesus painted a beautiful and challenging picture of what a disciple of His looks like. He said that His disciples love Him above all others (Luke 14:25–33), obey His commandments (John 14:15), abide in His Word (John 8:31), bear spiritual fruit (John 15:8), and are known by their love for one another (John 13:35). A disciple of Jesus is one who has been redeemed by Him, is being transformed into His image, worships Him, and lives on mission for Him—all while being a part of the community of Jesus, the church. Disciples are not fans of Jesus. They are not hobbyists, students, or even experts on the Savior. They are worshipers and followers, and this means they are necessarily theologians.

Despite what many excellent resources on theology suggest, theology is not simply the study of God. It includes the study of God as He is revealed in the Bible, but theology is incomplete if it is not both experienced and expressed.

The word *theology* comes from two Greek words: *theos* (God) and *logos* (words). Theology is the knowledge of God *articulated*. It is not meant to be personal in its scope, but communal. Theology should not be private, but public. The source of all theology is Scripture, but the purpose of theology is to make God known to all. Theology, therefore, should lead to worshiping God in spirit and truth.

A theologian, then, is one who knows God and makes Him known. To say that all Christians must be theologians is a bit incorrect. All Christians *are* theologians. They are either good or bad at being theologians, but all are theologians. All should be growing in theology, but it is impossible to be a Christian without engaging in the work of theology.

As a principle, *disciples are made when the people of God following the Son of God are instructed and transformed by the Word of God.* Apart from the ministry of the Word among the people of God, disciples cannot be made. To put it plainly, discipleship requires the church. Our hyper-individualistic culture offers customizable experiences that do not necessitate community. With the proliferation of Christian podcasts, conferences, books, and live-streaming worship events, many believers have come to see local congregations as supplemental to the life of faith, rather than critical to it.

It is the church that is made up of disciples of Jesus Christ, and it is the church that carries out the mission to continually make more disciples. The life of a disciple is inseparable from the local church. If we see this and believe this, we are then forced to address the issue of *how*. How does disciple-making work?

Most church growth experts today push the need for systems that help the church run efficiently, and programs to empower those systems. While systems and programs are helpful for making disciples, they are not enough.

I have found that it is helpful to think of church life, the context in which disciples are made, as encompassed in three environments. For ten years, I have been drawing out these three environments on napkins and whiteboards, using three different shapes to teach others in practical terms what the church does and how it does it. These environments are: the table, the pulpit, and the square. This is the big picture of how disciple-making is accomplished in and by the church.

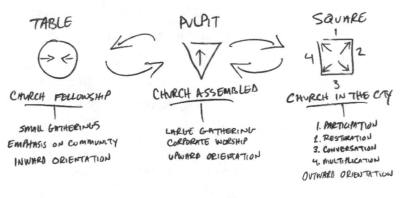

TABLE

CHURCH FELLOWSHIP

SMALL GATHERINGS
EMPHASIS ON COMMUNITY
INWARD ORIENTATION

PULPIT

CHURCH ASSEMBLED

LARGE GATHERING
CORPORATE WORSHIP
UPWARD ORIENTATION

SQUARE

CHURCH IN THE CITY

1. PARTICIPATION
2. RESTORATION
3. CONVERSATION
4. MULTIPLICATION
OUTWARD ORIENTATION

TABLE, PULPIT, SQUARE

The circle represents the environment cultivated in the smaller gatherings of a local church. I call this environment "the table" because these gatherings frequently take place around a coffee table, a dining room table, or a table elsewhere that facilitates gospel relationships. This environment often includes teaching, prayer, or outreach, but the real emphasis is on the building of relationships in which we are able to live out what God calls us to as disciples.

The triangle represents the larger, weekly gathering of a local church. I call this "the pulpit" because this is the place where God's people gather as one for corporate worship—to hear God's Word, to receive the ordinances, and to sing and confess with one voice the one and only Lord.

The square represents the "public square," where the church's presence in the culture is manifested through both informal and formal ministry. Church members participate in the culture wherever appropriate as good neighbors and light-bearers to those living in darkness. The church seeks the good of society through works of mercy, in which people in need experience the restoring power of God in the gospel. The church in the public square is not called to be silent, but rather to speak with those to whom they have been sent. From casual chats about common interests to the open-air preaching of the gospel in a local park, disciples speak up in their communities as ambassadors of Jesus Christ. And if healthy, local churches will work to see other churches started or revitalized; God wants His kingdom to advance and He wants His people to be active in more ways than simply being active members of a congregation.

These are the three essential environments in which disciples are made. Now, let's explore why each is vital and how they function.

PART 1

the TABLE

The environment of the table is where believers come together in smaller numbers than in most Sunday services. This is necessary because only in this context can believers experience aspects of church life in ways the New Testament prescribes but typically are not possible in corporate worship. From informal friendships and gatherings to organized small groups to the practice of hospitality, the local church can truly thrive only when its members gather around a table.

Chapter 1

OUR NEED FOR COMMUNITY

uman beings have been created by God to live in community. When God made Adam, He said, "It is not good that the man should be alone" (Gen. 2:18). This statement reflects man's need not only for a woman, but also for intimate relationships that cannot be found among other creatures.

People are not just hungry for community; they require it to truly live. This is not the result of some weakness found in humanity, but rather reflects the divine mark left upon every soul. We need community because we are made in the image of God, who has forever existed as Father, Son, and Holy Spirit. He has always known the love and harmony of communion within Himself. As people who bear His image, we are relational beings who need others like us with whom we can live life. And for Christians this is especially true. We need the love and harmony of the communion of saints. Without it, we will grow weak, and God's image will not shine as brightly in us as He intended.

SAVED TO COMMUNITY

But you are a chosen race, a royal priesthood, a holy nation, a people for his own possession, that you may proclaim the excellencies of him who called you out of darkness into his marvelous light. Once you were not a people, but now you are God's people; once you had not received mercy, but now you have received mercy.

(1 PETER 2:9–10)

When God saves sinners, He forgives their transgressions, cleanses them from all unrighteousness, and declares them to be righteous in Jesus Christ. Salvation includes receiving a new identity, heart, and spirit (Ezek. 36:26). But our redemption in Jesus Christ is not merely a rescue of the individual; it is a deliverance of a people from the domain of darkness into the kingdom of light, from friendship with the world into the family of God. We are saved by grace through faith into union with Christ and communion with His people (see 1 Cor. 12:13; Eph. 4). We are saved into the communion of the saints, where we find life and spiritual growth.

SANCTIFIED IN COMMUNITY

God promises to sanctify His people. This promise was prophesied in the Old Testament and realized in the New. God works in the soul of every Christian to grow them in faith and godliness. This inner transformation is the work of the Spirit through the ministry of the Word (see John 17:17; 2 Thess. 2:13). Just as we cannot be saved apart from the activity of the Spirit and the Word, neither can we experience spiritual growth apart from the Spirit and the Word. The work of the Spirit and the ministry of the Word are found and flourish in the church, and they are frequently intensely experienced in our personal relationships with other believers.

The community of faith is what forms and reforms the Christian. Believers are formed by the ongoing instruction of the Word and fellowship of believers in the church and are reformed by brothers and sisters who hold one another accountable through loving correction, reproof, and rebuke. Such accountability is effective only in a community where a common faith gives birth to mutual love.

SERVING IN COMMUNITY

For God has not destined us for wrath, but to
obtain salvation through our Lord Jesus Christ,
who died for us so that whether we are awake or

asleep we might live with him. Therefore encourage one another and build one another up, just as you are doing.

(1 THESS. 5:9–11)

The environment of our smaller gatherings and friendships in the church is where we can fulfill God's call on our lives. The people of God must meet together in smaller numbers to carry out the will of God in each other's lives.

For instance, if we gather together only on the Lord's Day for corporate worship, how can we possibly carry out the "one another" passages that pepper the New Testament? Apart from the environment of the table, it is impossible to truly

- "love one another with brotherly affection" (Rom. 12:10);
- "outdo one another in showing honor" (Rom. 12:10);
- "live in harmony with one another" (Rom. 12:16);
- "welcome one another as Christ welcomed you" (Rom. 15:7);
- "instruct one another" (Rom. 15:14);
- "have the same care for one another" (1 Cor. 12:25);

- "with all humility and gentleness, with patience, [bear] with one another in love" (Eph. 4:2);
- "be kind to one another, tenderhearted, forgiving one another, as God in Christ forgave you" (Eph. 4:32);
- "[submit] to one another out of reverence for Christ" (Eph 5:21);
- "stir up one another toward love and good works" (Heb. 10:24);
- "[encourage] one another" (Heb. 10:25);
- and "confess your sins to one another and pray for one another" (James 5:16).

We can do some of this only in part on Sunday mornings, but we can do it fully as we dwell in the environment of the table.

We need community because we were created for it. This means without community we cannot experience life as God intended. As God said, it is not good for anyone to be alone. Isolation is a consequence of the fall and a major reason many Christians flounder in the faith. It is only as we learn to live life together by faith that we can begin to understand the value of the church and experience the Christian life in its fullness.

Specific programs that help facilitate the ministry of service and meeting people's needs are good. But even more important to the life of the church is that we be people who are naturally caring for one another in ways that require sacrifice and thus result in bringing relief to those who need it. When one member or family of the church is served by others in tangible ways out of a sense of love from others, the environment of the table yields fruit. For this to happen, relationships are necessary. However, building a culture that helps these relationships to grow and remain strong requires the context of smaller gatherings and groups.

Chapter 2

SMALLER GROUPS

Church members have long practiced gathering together in smaller groups. Today, these gatherings are called "home groups," "community groups," "missional communities," or simply "small groups," among other names. Though they often have different emphases, the necessary component to healthy small groups is the fostering of a gospel-rich community where believers are cared for and challenged by one another.

The Puritans modeled this well in what they called "holy conference."[1] Holy conference amounted to a kind of small group. These groups were not a time for Christians just to socialize. Nor was it a time simply to study the Bible together. Those who attended conference did both, to be sure. But their time together was devoted to something even deeper. These Christians intended on applying the truths of Scripture to each individual's life.

In conference, church members regularly engaged

one another in discussions on biblical texts as it related to the spiritual state of their souls. This required honesty, transparency, and trust from each individual, which is difficult to practice today in our individualistic society but can nevertheless thrive in the environment of the table. These Christians used Scripture passages related to their pastors' previous sermon, their own notes on those sermons, or from their own private Bible reading.

These smaller gatherings provided the context in which exhortation and encouragement happened naturally. Yes, these gatherings were more "inward" than "outward" in that they focused on those members gathered together and their relationship with God. God calls all believers to gospel-centered fellowship, and this is what readies us for better service to one another and those outside of the church.

Theologian Joanne Jung summarizes the benefits of conference: "The profitability of conference was clear: enhanced biblical understanding, the warming of the soul, and even a greater desire for the Word."[2] Like the Sunday gatherings, these were groups of mixed company, not divided by age or sex. Jung explains,

> Evidence shows that the advantages of gathering in small groups to discuss biblical passages as they relate to life experiences were extensive and were not limited to any one particular group of people. There was no

gender, literacy, or class distinction. In conference there would be no discrimination.[3]

This is different from age or gender segregated Sunday School instruction—which no doubt can be a helpful component of disciple making—in that these small groups were more intimate, relational, and participatory, making the most of the "communion of the saints."

"Communion of saints" is not a phrase we use much today, outside of reciting The Apostles' Creed, which says, "I believe in . . . the communion of saints." But our salvation and sanctification are experienced in such communion. The Heidelberg Catechism unpacks this in question 55:

Q. What do you understand by *the communion of saints*?

A. First, that believers, all and everyone, as members of Christ have communion with him and share in all his treasures and gifts. Second, that everyone is duty-bound to use his gifts readily and cheerfully for the benefit and well-being of the other members.[4]

Smaller groups, whatever we call them, must prioritize Scripture, persevere in prayer, and aim at strengthening each other's faith and Christian friendship. Whether in weekly small groups or occasional seminars, the church should offer biblical and theological instruction in this environment, which allows for questions and answers.

From organized small groups to the ongoing friendships that mark the whole of our lives, the essential aspect of this environment is the building of Christian community, which in turn helps to build healthy churches.

Believers ought to read the Word and pray together, but we should also work and play together. I am always thrilled when I see the people in formal community groups from our church go to the movies, a sporting event, or a restaurant together—when they fellowship together without an agenda or a plan, when spending time together is natural and rewarding. These interactions, too, are critical for building godly community.

Chapter 3

HOSPITALITY

ospitality is often treated as an issue of manners. We believe we should be hospitable because it is the polite thing to do. Worse than that, many of us claim to be introverts and give ourselves a pass on the practice. But according to Scripture, hospitality is not a matter of manners; it is about mission. Scripture calls all Christians to this practice: "Show hospitality to one another without grumbling" (1 Peter 4:9).

TREATING OUTSIDERS LIKE INSIDERS

The biblical concept of hospitality leads us to treat outsiders like insiders because we, who once were outsiders ourselves, have been welcomed into God's kingdom and made to be insiders. The call to treat outsiders like insiders spans both Testaments in Scripture, making it both a privilege and a responsibility.

For example, in Leviticus 19:34, God commanded

Israel to "treat the stranger who sojourns with you as the native among you, and you shall love him as yourself, for you were strangers in the land of Egypt: I am the LORD your God." Israel knew what it was like to be a stranger, unknown and unwelcome, and then to find God's grace, which brought them near to Him. They learned a profound truth in their salvation: God welcomes outsiders.

God wants His people to extend the same sort of welcoming to others. As members of Christ's body, we are called to "contribute to the needs of the saints and seek to show hospitality" (Rom. 12:13) and to do so "without grumbling" (1 Peter 4:9). But like Israel, our calling to hospitality is not a response to social needs and expectations, but rather an outpouring of what we have experienced in Jesus Christ. God called us to Himself when we were strangers to His promises, and He made us, who were not His people, a people for His own possession (1 Peter 2:9–10). In the gospel, Jesus welcomes not the perfect or the free, but the broken and the burdened. As He has accepted each of us, so we must accept others into our lives.

INSIDE AND OUTSIDE THE CHURCH

This is first a call to draw near to one another inside the church on the basis of our common faith, salvation, and

Lord. Building friendships can be difficult for many Christians. Some people feel awkward reaching out to others they do not know, and some groups of friends can quickly become cliques as a result of the comfort and familiarity found within.

Healthy churches create an invitational culture where the people go far beyond warm welcomes at Sunday services to a genuine embrace of outsiders and newcomers into both the life of the church and their own personal lives.

The gospel calls us to be hospitable not only to those in the community of faith, but also to those still of the world. We see this in Jesus' Parable of the Good Samaritan:

> Jesus replied, "A man was going down from Jerusalem to Jericho, and he fell among robbers, who stripped him and beat him and departed, leaving him half dead. Now by chance a priest was going down that road, and when he saw him he passed by on the other side. So likewise a Levite, when he came to the place and saw him, passed by on the other side. But a Samaritan, as he journeyed, came to where he was, and when he saw him, he had compassion. He went to him and bound up his wounds, pouring on oil and wine. Then he set him on his own animal and brought him to an inn and took care of him. And the next day he took out two denarii and gave them to the innkeeper, saying,

> *'Take care of him, and whatever more you spend, I*
> *will repay you when I come back.' Which of these*
> *three, do you think, proved to be a neighbor to the*
> *man who fell among the robbers?" He said, "The*
> *one who showed him mercy." And Jesus said to him,*
> *"You go, and do likewise."*

(LUKE 10:30–37)

When Jesus is asked "Who is my neighbor?" he turns the tables on the one asking the question and essentially says, "Those around you, even those unlike you or whom you may not like. They are your neighbors. And your role as their neighbor is to practice hospitality."

Hospitality is not simply inviting guests to your house, but welcoming people into your life, often at great cost to your own comfort, time, and plans. In sum, hospitality is service to, interest in, and compassion for others.

A CULTURE OF INVITATION AND INVESTMENT

In one sense, biblical hospitality calls the believer to invite others into his or her life, but in another sense it calls the Christian to step into the lives of others—for their good. The Christian in the world is an ambassador of Jesus Christ, sent to bear witness to our resurrected Lord in both word and deed. This calling to bear witness is powerfully felt relationally when we follow the lead of Jesus in seeking out others to serve.

Hospitality is essential to the environment of the table because it is the beginning of all gospel relationships, and often the beginning of the gospel taking root in the lives of those who are strangers to God.

Hospitality is the result of and is shaped by one's own faith and it is worked out in their own circle of influence or opportunity. Your church is one such circle. You know those who are your friends, those with whom you regularly speak and spend time. You sit with them at Sunday services and notice when they are missing. But in that same church are others you have yet to notice or welcome into your life. Hospitality can change that.

This is too often thought of exclusively as bringing non-Christians or people unknown into our lives, but it should also be the common practice of believers to know one another and share their lives together.

Your church, your job, your gym, your school, and many other places are different circles of opportunity and influence where you are expected by God to bless others with the grace of hospitality. The table is an environment that has more of an inward emphasis. Outreach is one necessary aspect to it. But in the end, the goal of this environment is to build and strengthen Christian community.

The table is a necessary environment of church life.

Some so value this environment they believe this environment alone is enough for the church. But more is needed. Without living out our faith within the context of the table, we cannot be or do what God calls us to be and do. Without it a church will find itself anemic. But if we do not also have the environment of the pulpit as central to church life, we cease to be a church altogether.

PART 2

the PULPIT

Central in the diagram of table, pulpit, and square is the triangle, the environment of corporate worship. This is the church's central and largest gathering where God's people meet together to receive the Word and ordinances. All three environments are critical to the life of a local church, but none is more important than corporate worship. This gathering on the first day of the week is the brightest reflection of the kingdom of God in the world today. Edmund Clowney writes,

> Above all, we must prize the blessing of corporate worship. The church of the Lord, gathered for worship, marks the pinnacle of our fellowship with the Lord and with one another. The church is the people

of God, the new humanity, the beginning of the new creation, a colony of heaven. . . In corporate worship we experience the meaning of union with Christ.[1]

We call this environment the pulpit because the ministry of the Word is central to corporate worship.

Chapter 4

CORPORATE WORSHIP

In the beginning, God created the world and all that is in it. He created man and woman in His own image and for the purpose of glorifying Him, both individually and together. God has created humanity to worship Him together, as a people of faith. Worshiping God is the appropriate response of creatures made in His image, for not only are we made to worship, but the Lord is truly worthy of worship.

> Ascribe to the LORD, O heavenly beings,
>   ascribe to the LORD glory and strength.
> Ascribe to the LORD the glory due his name;
>   worship the LORD in the splendor of holiness.
>
> (PS. 29:1–2)

The word *worship* comes from the Old English word *worth-ship,* meaning "to ascribe worth and honor to another." We worship the Lord when we recognize Him as worthy of all honor and glory, ascribe Him such worth, and live in a manner worthy of His name (Ps. 29; Eph. 4:1; Col. 1:10).

Worship, therefore, takes different forms: private worship when we are alone with the Lord reading His Word and praying; family worship when the whole household is gathered together to seek Him; and corporate worship on the Lord's Day. And running through and beyond all of this is the life of worship Paul calls us to in Romans 12:1: "I appeal to you therefore, brothers, by the mercies of God, to present your bodies as a living sacrifice, holy and acceptable to God, which is your spiritual worship."

But what I have in mind as we consider the environment of the pulpit is specifically corporate worship within the local church.

CORPORATE WORSHIP

I love corporate worship. Since my conversion in my late teens, I have always been excited to get to church on Sunday and sing God's praises, hear His Word, and pray with His people. Of course, this does not mean I have always been excited to go to a particular church. But I have always loved worship done well.

I have worshiped with all kinds of churches. I have been with tiny congregations where worship made me exult in the joy of our risen Savior, and I have worshiped with large congregations that left me wishing I had stayed in bed that morning. Of course, I've also experienced this the other way around.

My wife and I once attended a small Reformed Baptist church. The building was plain-Jane. No cool lights hung in the sanctuary. They had no worship pastor, no choir, and no instruments. Yet their gathering was truly powerful, and I found myself worshiping in spirit and truth. Why?

On the one hand, they had all the essential elements needed for corporate worship. Yes, some things are required: the Word of God read and preached, the prayers and songs of God's people lifted up in the name of Jesus Christ, and the ordinances of baptism and the Lord's Supper rightly administered. But simply having these elements in place is not enough. These must be carried out with focus, a sense of depth, clarity, passion, and purpose.

Focus

The focus of the gathered church is the Lord Jesus Christ and His work of salvation—accomplished through His life, death, and resurrection—for all who believe.

Corporate worship should be distinctly Christian, incapable of being confused with another cause, movement, or religion.

A proper focus on Jesus means that the whole gathering should work to lead everyone present to "see" Jesus. This means every aspect of the gathering, every part of the liturgy, should be designed to help us draw near to Christ by faith. Whatever is not helping us move toward Him needs to be cut.

Depth

Worship that is powerful gains its strength from the heralding of the glories of our triune God. This means that our worship must be intentionally and deeply theological. If we are God's people, saved and gathered together to "proclaim the excellencies of him" (1 Peter 2:9), then we must not only know them, but also make them known. Worship that does not revel in the character and work of our sovereign and saving God will lift up something or someone else instead.

Clarity

Deep worship is crucial, but without clarity it will prove fruitless. Our gatherings must be Christ-centered and comprehensible. The words we use in every aspect of our worship must be defined. When we consider the style of our worship music and the nature of the environment in which we gather, we must be careful not to first ask, "Will the culture like this or not?" Rather, our main question should be, "Is this biblical?" Only then can we begin to answer other important questions like, "Will the people understand what we are saying and doing?" or, "Will this help us lead them to the gospel?" Our goal should be for people to encounter biblical truth in an accessible manner in every aspect of the service.

Passion

Worship should be felt. Our affections should be stirred when we gather to sing with one voice the praises of our one Lord. If our singing, praying, reading, and preaching are not earnest, why would we be surprised if the congregation is listless? We need more than eloquent speakers with clever sermons. We need men filled with the Spirit, fueled by faith, who passionately proclaim the good news we all so desperately need. We need more than just accomplished musicians at the front of the sanctuary. We need congregations so full of the joy of salvation that they cannot help but sing—and sing loudly.

Purpose

People often get overly concerned with the "target audience" of the worship gathering. Is the service aimed at the unconverted person walking into our midst, or should we target believers for their edification? I think both emphases miss the mark. Our target in worship is God Himself. We want first to please Him, to worship His way for His glory. We then want to reveal Him, to make Him known to the people gathered, as we give everyone the opportunity to draw near to Him in faith and repentance, to see Him as Lord over all. The purpose of our worship is the glory of God. Knowing *why* we gather and for *whom* we gather leads to both evangelism and edification in our gathering.

WHERE WE LOOK IN CORPORATE WORSHIP

When a healthy church gathers on Sunday, God's Word will be read and preached, the ordinances will be administered, prayers will be lifted up, and all will join a chorus of others who herald the good news by singing psalms, hymns, and spiritual songs to God and one another. But where should we look? This might seem like a strange question, but allow me to tell you where to set your gaze.

Look Up

> *Set your minds on things that are above, not on things that are on earth. For you have died, and your life is hidden with Christ in God.*
>
> (COL. 3:2–3).

Worship is about God, not us. Everything in the service should direct our thoughts upward to our reigning Savior. If you find distractions or deficiencies in your church's gathering, exercise self-control and guide your own thoughts toward the excellency of Jesus. If the preacher is not pointing you to Jesus in the text from which he preaches, search Him out yourself. Commit yourself to seeking the Lord when you gather on the Lord's Day. This is your responsibility, and no one can prevent you from seeking Him.

Look In

> *Search me, O God, and know my heart! Try me and know my thoughts! And see if there be any grievous way in me, and lead me in the way everlasting!*
>
> (PS. 139:23–24)

While worship is fundamentally about God, we cannot help but come to a better understanding of ourselves as we come to know Him. As you sing of His holiness, justice, goodness, and truth; and meditate on the life, death, and resurrection of Jesus; be sure to examine your own heart. Are you addressing your own sins? What must you do? What must you grab ahold of by faith? Be receptive to the convicting work of the Holy Spirit and to the ministry of the Word. How do you need to repent, what do you need to believe, and in what truth will you delight?

Look Around

> Be filled with the Spirit, addressing one another in
> psalms and hymns and spiritual songs, singing and
> making melody to the Lord with your heart.

(EPH. 5:18–19)

The direction of corporate worship is primarily vertical—directed toward God—yet it is also horizontal. The people around you are part of the family of God; they are your brothers and sisters. Do you know them? Do you serve them? How can you encourage them in their faith and life? Do you understand that this is part of your calling? Do you know that God expects you to minister to them in ways that extend beyond the timeframe of Sunday worship? As you worship Christ together, you should grow in your affection for His people, who are now, because of Jesus, your people.

Look Back

> I will ponder all your work, and meditate on your
> mighty deeds.

(PS. 77:12)

When the service is over and you head out to lunch or back home to rest, be sure to look back on what you sang, prayed, and heard. Talk about it with others and take those truths even further into your own heart. Now is the time to continue preaching that message to yourself, pressing on to see what God will do in and through you. I believe half of the reason we get little out of corporate worship is we leave everything we received back in the assembly when in fact God wants us to take it with us wherever we go.

Corporate worship is central to the Christian life, but for us to make the most of it, we must enter into it intentionally and carefully, seeking to worship God in spirit and truth.

Chapter 5

THE WORD IN WORSHIP

The environment of the pulpit is named after the formal ministry of the Word in gathered worship. This is not to suggest that the ordinances are not essential, or that the psalms, hymns, and spiritual songs are unimportant. I use the term *pulpit* to emphasize the truth that corporate worship is *formed* and *filled* by Scripture. This is the primary context where instruction and teaching take place, but much more than teaching happens in our weekly gatherings.

SCRIPTURE FORMS OUR WORSHIP

In corporate worship, many churches today mix God-ordained means of grace and inventive practices that are neither warranted by Scripture nor helpful for our growth in faith. While worship services should look and sound different in various cultures, cities, and contexts, their essential practices should look the same.

There are two differing views on what the church can and should do when gathered for worship on the Lord's Day. The "normative principle" says the church is bound to do what Scripture prescribes but is free to implement other practices so long as they do not contradict Scripture's teaching. The "regulative principle" teaches that the essential elements of corporate worship are prescribed in Scripture, and that whatever is not implicitly or explicitly given in Scripture should be avoided. While good churches may wind up adopting one view over another, I believe the best option is to adhere rigorously to what we find in Scripture while following the regulative principle.

Even among those who hold to the regulative principle, disagreements abound regarding what is and is not permissible. But what all who hold this view agree on is that corporate worship should not be formed by anything without scriptural warrant.

The Bible gives commands and examples for us to follow in developing our practices in corporate worship. Worship services must include the reading and preaching of God's Word (1 Tim. 4:13; 2 Tim. 4:2); the proper administration of the ordinances (Matt. 28:19; Acts 2:38–39; 1 Cor. 11:23–26; Col. 2:11–12);

the singing of psalms, hymns, and spiritual songs (Eph. 5:19; Col. 3:16); prayer (Matt. 21:13; Ps. 134:2); and an offering taken up for the work of ministry (1 Cor. 16:2; 2 Cor. 9:6–7). These are the essential elements of worship in the church and should come to form the gathering. While they may look different from church to church, the essentials should remain in place. There is not room for inventive practices that move the church gathering away from these God-given directives.

Some wonder if this regulative principle hinders the church from making accommodations to the culture or the people who are being led in worship. Are we forbidden from using projected lyrics on a screen, or must we use a hymnal? Are chairs out, and pews in? Is a pulpit appropriate? And if Scripture alone dictates what we do in worship, how do we handle these other aspects of worship?

Christians who embrace the regulative principle distinguish between things "essential" and things "accidental." The essential elements of worship are given to us in the Word of God, but the handling of such essentials is often seen as accidental, or circumstantial. The time of worship, the length of worship, and the way we handle the elements of worship should be determined thoughtfully as a means of best carrying out God's directives.

As the 1689 Baptist Confessions articulates,

> But the acceptable way of worshiping the true God, is instituted by himself, and so limited by his own revealed will, that he may not be worshipped according to the imagination and devices of men, nor the suggestions of Satan, under any visible representations, or any other way not prescribed in the Holy Scriptures.[1]

This deals with the elements of worship. But the Confession also says that

> there are some circumstances concerning the worship of God, and government of the church, common to human actions and societies, which are to be ordered by the light of nature and Christian prudence, according to the general rules of the Word, which are always to be observed.[2]

All this may seem nitpicky, but God has always cared about how He is worshiped, and we should as well. Consider Cain's worship, which was found unacceptable to God. Or Nadab and Abihu, who offered "unauthorized fire" in worship to the Lord. They disregarded the Lord's commands for worship, and the consequences are terrifying:

> Now Nadab and Abihu, the sons of Aaron, each took his censer and put fire in it and laid incense on it and offered unauthorized fire before the LORD, which he had not commanded them. And fire came out from before the LORD and consumed

*them, and they died before the LORD. Then Moses
said to Aaron, "This is what the LORD has said:
'Among those who are near me I will be sanctified,
and before all the people I will be glorified.'" And
Aaron held his peace.*

(LEV. 10:1–3)

This does not mean that God kills people today for disregarding His commands for worship. But it does communicate to us that following God's commands, which were given for our good, is a serious matter.

The question is: Who will determine how we worship God as the church? Does the church decide what is acceptable, or does God? While there is liberty in the circumstances of our corporate worship, the elements of worship are regulated by Scripture. The Word of God forms our worship.

SCRIPTURE FILLS OUR WORSHIP

The environment of the pulpit is not only formed by the Word, but also filled with the Word. It is commonly said that in the worship of the church the Word is read and preached, prayed and sung, and seen.

The reading of God's Word in corporate worship has been evaporating for some time. In many churches today, all that remains of the Word read aloud to the congregation is a verse or two at the opening of the service.

But the command to read the Word publicly (1 Tim. 4:13) is not a call to nod to it in passing. It is a call to read it thoughtfully and thoroughly.

Reading Scripture in worship is not merely a call to give attention, but a call to hear God's revelation of Himself. For it to be read thoughtfully and thoroughly requires us to read the revelation of God's person and work by which people might be confronted, convicted, and comforted. Readings from the Old Testament and the New Testament ought to be common. Longer and multiple readings should mark the whole of the service as the church is led through its liturgy. The law of God should show us our sin, and the gospel of God should show us our Savior. And in it all, the church is called to respond to God in faith and repentance.

The preaching of the Word is not accomplished by spring-boarding from one text into a talk divorced from the text or the theology of the text. The preaching of the Word requires ministers to open the Word, explain it, expound upon it, and apply it—all while leading us to Jesus as Lord. While preachers will vary in style and mannerism, their shared approach ought to be the clear communication of Scripture so that the church might grow in its understanding and experience of God.

The Word must also be prayed in corporate worship. Prayer is not only a congregation's appeal to God for what it lacks or needs, but also its praise based on who God is and what He has done. This means that proper prayer is necessarily grounded in the Word, for there we see God and His promises. The Word is prayed in adoration, confession, supplication, and thanksgiving. Prayer should be offered not only at the beginning, the end, and during the offering, but also throughout the service in various ways. It should not be used as a time of transitioning between elements of worship—in which the band or anyone else is given ample time to sneak up front for whatever comes next—but should be an essential element to worship.

The Word must also be sung in worship. The psalms, hymns, and spiritual songs we sing may be taken directly from Scripture, or they may more creatively reflect particular truths of Scripture. Still, all a church sings should emerge from the Word of God in such a way that God is made known.

The Word is seen in the ordinances. In baptism and the Lord's Supper, the gospel is preached. In baptism, we see one who has been cleansed of sin by the blood of Christ. Not only that, we see them buried with Christ as they are plunged beneath the water and then raised up in new life with Him as they emerge from the water. In the Lord's Supper, we see the body of Jesus broken and His blood spilled for us. The bread and the wine are symbols of the gospel that saves. In both ordinances, the Word of God, specifically the gospel, is displayed for all to see.

SCRIPTURE REVEALS GOD

The reason God's Word is so integral to and essential for corporate worship is that by it we know God, see ourselves as we truly are, and rightly understand our circumstances in light of both of these truths.

The Bible is not a collection of stories or a manual for morality. It contains stories, historical narratives, poetry, epistles, prophecies, and more. But these are not what ultimately characterize the Bible. All these were included so that that we might better know who God is. God has gone to great lengths to teach us about Himself by condescending to our level, by speaking to us in ways we can understand. He even goes beyond this by using multiple genres of literature, allowing us to access the truth from different vantage points.

Who is God and what is He like? This knowledge can come to us only through Scripture. For what is known of God in creation is not only far more limited than what Scripture reveals, but it is also universally rejected by us all.

When we encounter God's Word, we are awed by His holiness, humbled by His grace, comforted by His goodness, and strengthened by His love. God reveals His character so we might properly respond to Him in faith, love, and obedience. Who is God? He says of Himself:

> The LORD, the LORD, a God merciful and gracious, slow to anger, and abounding in steadfast love and faithfulness, keeping steadfast love for thousands, forgiving iniquity and transgression and sin, but who will by no means clear the guilty, visiting the iniquity of the fathers on the children and the children's children, to the third and the fourth generation.
>
> (EX. 34:6–7)

Scripture reveals to us not only who God is, but also what He does. By Scripture we know that God is the Creator and Sustainer of all things, that He in His providence orchestrates every detail of human history and experience, and that He is working all things together for the good of those who love Him. We know that God is sovereign, just, merciful, and patient.

All of this is important because the Word, in revealing the person and work of God, is then able to adjust our skewed perspective in life. In Psalm 73, Asaph expresses his frustration at the ease of life experienced by the wicked and at the affliction that oppresses the righteous. He was haunted by the seeming unfairness of life, and he began to question the truth he had always known: that God is good to His people. As he wrestled with how things appeared to him in this broken world, he began to think that believing in and following the Lord is a waste of time. But when Asaph walked into the sanctuary, into the place of worship, he understood. His vision was corrected. You can see how intensely his faith was tested:

> All in vain have I kept my heart clean
>   and washed my hands in innocence.
> For all the day long I have been stricken
>   and rebuked every morning.
> If I had said, "I will speak thus,"
>   I would have betrayed the generation of your
>   children.
>
> But when I thought how to understand this,
>   it seemed to me a wearisome task,
> until I went into the sanctuary of God;
>   then I discerned their end.

(PS. 73:13–17)

The revelation of God in the context of worship helped him see reality, not just with his eyes. Though the wicked prosper now, their end is destruction. The righteous may suffer now, but God is with them and for them, and He will eventually vindicate them. Near the end of the psalm, Asaph's perspective is changed, though his circumstances remained the same:

When my soul was embittered,
  when I was pricked in heart,
I was brutish and ignorant;
  I was like a beast toward you.

Nevertheless, I am continually with you;
  you hold my right hand.
You guide me with your counsel,
  and afterward you will receive me to glory.
Whom have I in heaven but you?
  And there is nothing on earth that I desire besides
    you.
My flesh and my heart may fail,
  but God is the strength of my heart and my
    portion forever.

(PS. 73:21–26)

SCRIPTURE REFORMS OUR HEARTS

Scripture is so critical to the corporate worship of the church because it also changes our hearts. God's Word transforms the believer (Rom. 12:2).

This transformation is the recreation of a man or woman that begins the moment he or she is born again, continues throughout his or her life progressively, and is gloriously completed when Christ returns (2 Cor. 5:17; 1 Thess. 4:3–5; 5:23; 1 Pet. 1–2; 1 John 3:2–3). The theological term for this ongoing change is *sanctification*.

Sanctification is not so much about becoming more religious, but more human. It is the restoring of the image of God in us that was marred by sin. It is the life-long process in which God conforms us to the image of His Son. God does this work in us by the ministry of the Word through the power of the Spirit.

In John 17:17, Jesus prayed to the Father for His people—every Christian—that we would be changed: "Sanctify them in truth; your word is truth." It is by the Word read, preached, sang, and seen that we are sanctified. Worship, when it is biblical, lifts up God in glory and consequently lifts up the Christian from sin.

Sanctification is not the process by which we learn how to behave. It is much more than behavior modification. It is an internal transformation of the soul by the Holy Spirit that produces a changed life bearing the fruit of the Spirit (Gal. 5:22–23). Sanctification is a becoming of what we were designed to be.

SCRIPTURE LEADS US INTO COMMUNION WITH GOD

Worship is, in a sense, a meeting with God. God draws near to us as we draw near to Him (James 4:8). As His people, we are intended to have communion, an intimate relationship characterized by love, with the Lord (1 John 1:3). And this happens as the Word works in us.

The Holy Spirit uses Scripture to show us the glory of God and our own sin. We are convicted and see our need for grace; faith then leads us to run to Jesus Christ. The revelation of God in His Word compels us to move closer to God, even in the painful awareness of our guilt, without fear of judgment. For in Christ we are pardoned and accepted. The Word lights the path that leads us to the shelter of God's grace where we find divine love, protection, and true fellowship.

Communion with God is possible only through Jesus Christ. The ministry of the Word, therefore, must always lead us to the gospel, or it is an incomplete ministry that will produce neither real change nor true intimacy with God.

Chapter 6

WORSHIPING IN SPIRIT AND TRUTH

Corporate worship on the Lord's Day is precious to the people of God. We are invited to gather together for fellowship with God and one another through the Word, ordinances, prayer, and song. Jesus said true worshipers worship God in "spirit and truth" (John 4:23–24). This indicates two things for all Christians and churches.

First, true worshipers worship sincerely by faith ("in spirit"). They are not hypocrites who pretend to be what they are not. They do not deny their sin, but confess it. They are not ashamed of the gospel; rather, they proclaim it. True worshipers know who they are by nature (sinners) and who they are by grace (saints) and that they are now truly free to worship.

Second, true worshipers worship God according to God's revealed will ("in truth"). Though free to express themselves in many different ways when worshiping, they are careful to worship God according to the practices and principles He has revealed in Scripture. True worshipers do not strive for invention in worship, but faithfulness (see chapter 5).

Yet even when we agree on all this, worshiping on Sundays can be trying for us. We are busy people, and many of us show up to the Sunday gathering tired from a week of labor and activities. For families with children, just getting out the door on time can be a challenge, if not a battle. And when we finally sit down in church, we are assaulted with distractions emerging from our own hearts and minds.

Worshiping in spirit and truth sounds good in theory, but it does not always come easy in practice. In order to worship in spirit and truth, we must prepare ourselves, actively participate in the service, and then reflect on the service afterward.

PREPARE

The significance of corporate worship must not be overlooked. We are not gathered to observe a show or attend a lecture. We gather to worship the living God, to draw near to Him through Jesus Christ by feasting on His Word, repenting of our sin, and rejoicing in His salvation. In order to receive the most we can in worship, it is wise for us to prepare our hearts the night before.

Prayer is the primary means by which we prepare our hearts for worship. We should be in prayer for those who will lead as well as for all who attend, asking God to draw people to the Son, to revive the lukewarm by His Spirit, and to penetrate hearts with His Word.

And of course, you must pray for your own soul, confessing your sin and trusting in the pardon that the Father gives in Jesus. We ought to ask God to show us any wretched ways in our hearts and to speak to our fears and needs when we gather in the assembly. In his outstanding little book *The Christian's Daily Walk*, seventeenth-century English minister and devotional writer Henry Scudder explained the place of prayer in preparation for worship:

> Then pray for yourself, and for the minister, that God would give him a mouth to speak, and you a heart to hear, as you both ought to do. All this, before you shall assemble for public worship.[1]

It is also helpful to read and meditate on the passage that your pastor will be preaching from on Sunday. Early on in my first church plant, a man named Mark called my cellphone, which at the time was also the church's official phone line. He told me he was in town with his son and would be joining us for worship the next day.

He wanted to know what passage I would be preaching from so he and his son could read it and pray through it together that night. The next day, Mark and his son showed up to our little church plant and were prepared to worship our risen Savior. I had no idea that I had been on the phone with Pastor Mark Dever of Capitol Hill Baptist Church in Washington, D.C.! His example is one we all would do well to follow.

Another means of preparation is rest. The often unnecessarily hectic pace of our lives can make transitioning to worship on the Lord's Day difficult. Be sure to get enough sleep the night before. Fatigue can greatly hinder your participation in worship. On Sunday morning, be sure to get up early enough so you will not be rushed. When you arrive at church, be ready to respond to what the Lord will do.

PARTICIPATE

Getting the most out of corporate worship requires you to do more than show up. You must participate in the act of worship in all of its forms. You are not an observer, but a worshiper. The only observer is the Lord Himself who receives our offering with delight through His Son, Jesus Christ.

Arrive at the service early. Sometimes, in God's providence, we all arrive late, but our habit should be to arrive early. Getting there before the service begins not only allows us to participate in the whole gathering, but also gives us the opportunity to fellowship with and serve others. The call to worship that formally begins the assembly is not a bell that merely announces the beginning of an event, but an invitation to direct our hearts upward toward our triune God. The first verses of Scripture that are read are selected by careful planning and God's providence. Arriving late means you will miss something good that God has for you.

Hear the Word with eagerness and receive it with gladness. The reading of Scripture in worship is the very voice of God, and we must be ready to listen to Him. Here, the Lord speaks to His people collectively and to you individually. Distractions will abound, so we must consciously fight them to give God our full attention. Whenever the Word of God is read it is, as seventeenth-century Puritan preacher Richard Steele explains, an "audible conference of the Almighty with your soul. A distraction lets him talk unto the walls."[2]

Sing with your heart to the Lord and to those present. Scripture commands us to address "one another in psalms and hymns and spiritual songs, singing and making melody to the Lord with your heart" (Eph. 5:19). It is painfully obvious that in many churches today, much of the congregation lip-syncs along with the band on stage. Even if the entire body were to sing aloud, it would be impossible to hear them over the vocalists and musicians. But the Lord calls us to sing to Him and to one another. This is a form of worship that God has specifically prescribed for us. Yes, we sing with our hearts, but such songs are to be amplified by faith and run through the speakers of our mouths. Here is where the real volume should come from. We should be turned up as far as we can be.

There may be songs you are not fond of, to be sure. If the melody is not to your liking, focus on the words, assuming they reflect the truth of God and the gospel. Do not allow your preferences to short-circuit your worship of God. This gathering is not set to meet your tastes, but the tastes of Almighty God.

Pray with those who lead in prayer. It is easy to tune out when someone else is leading in prayer. So keep in mind that this is not the time for one person to pray, but for all God's people to pray. Push distractions out of your mind to give attention to what is being offered up by the one and echo those prayers in your own heart, adding to them as you and the rest of the church entreat the Lord together. Again, Steele writes, "Prayer is a pouring out the heart unto the Lord; by a distraction you pour it aside."[3]

Follow the preacher. When the preacher delivers

the sermon, work diligently to follow him closely with your Bible in hand, ready to receive the message—not as man's word, but as God's Word (1 Thess. 1:6; 2:13). If you have a difficult time following the preacher, keep your Bible open and search it prayerfully. When you read the Word of God, you are "perusing . . . God's heart in black and white, where you may believe every letter to be written in blood."[4]

Let the various parts of corporate worship draw you to our triune God. In our weakness, or sometimes in the weakness of a particular element of the service, we may not experience much grace in the moment. If the songs do not enflame your heart, then perhaps the sermon will. Or if the sermon is difficult for you to digest, perhaps the prayers will lift your heart in adoration. God is at work in each element of worship, so each component—the call to worship, songs, prayers, preaching, Lord's Supper, offering, and benediction—has the ability to challenge and change you.

And when the service is over, go as one who is sent. When you return home, remember that you are not simply leaving, but are sent by God to believe and embody His Word, walk in the Spirit, and testify to the reality of Jesus Christ in all of life.

Finally, when the assembly has been sent out and you are alone or with family or friends, reflect on what was heralded. Return to the Word that was preached, discuss it with others, and ask God to continue working in you what He said that day.

There is much to be gained in corporate worship, but I find that we easily miss out when we are not prepared for it, participating in it, or reflecting on it. As Scudder noted,

> Do all this the rather, because there is not a clearer sign to distinguish you from one that is profane, than this, of conscientiously keeping holy the Lord's day. Neither is there any ordinary means of gaining strength and growth of grace in the inward man like this, of due observing the sabbath. For this is God's great mart or fair-day for the soul, on which you may buy of Christ wine, milk, bread, marrow and fatness, gold, white raiment, eye salve, — even all things which are necessary, and which will satisfy, and cause the soul to live. It is the special day of proclaiming and sealing of pardons to penitent sinners. It is God's special day of publishing and sealing your patent of eternal life. It is a blessed day, sanctified for all these blessed purposes.[5]

Corporate worship is one of the primary means by which disciples are made. It is not a show to observe, nor an event to attend. It is centerpiece of the Christian life where God's people gather together as one ascribing glory to our great God. The whole of corporate worship revolves around the Word of God. Here the Word is read, preached, prayed, sung, and seen. It not only forms and fills the service, but also forms the souls of God's people. While the ministry of the Word is seen in the lives of all God's people in a variety of ways, its presence in corporate worship is where it is seen most beautifully and powerfully.

—

Chapter 7

LITURGY

To many, "liturgy" sounds like something you would find in the Roman Catholic Mass. But every church has a liturgy. A liturgy is the order and arrangement of a worship service. I have preached in small rural churches that have a simple service, and they still have a liturgy. It would contain one reading of Scripture, three songs, one prayer, a sermon, and an offering.

The issue I want to address is not whether a church will have a liturgy, but whether it will develop a biblically sound, theologically rich liturgy that helps lead people into worship. A good liturgy will walk the congregation through the full experience of Christian faith—from guilt to grace to gratitude. We need to see the reality and ruin of our sin, know the love of God and the redemption we have through Jesus' death and resurrection, and respond in joyful gratitude to the Lord for what He has done for us.

In seeing and sensing our guilt before God we are best prepared to rest in the grace of God that justifies the sinner. His grace cleanses the filthy, makes the immoral righteous, and reconciles rebels to God. Grace received results in gratitude expressed in joyful song, bold proclamation, and careful obedience.

There is no biblically mandated liturgy that all churches must follow, but I have come to greatly value the liturgy of the church I serve at. We use a basic liturgical order (it is not original to us) that helps us as a congregation look and respond to God, His law, and His gospel. Our liturgy consists of eight basic components.

Revelation

Each worship gathering begins with a reading from Scripture that highlights the character and work of God. God has revealed Himself in His Word, and this self-revelation of God is our starting point. After the passage is read, a prayer is offered.

Adoration

Revelation leads us into adoration, or words of praise to God, that includes songs, more Scripture, more prayers, and corporate or responsive readings. This is a time of marveling at God's goodness.

Confession

We cannot see the beauty and goodness of God without also seeing the ugliness of our sin. So adoration leads us into a time of confession. This always includes a pastoral prayer, but may also contain a responsive reading that focuses on guilt, repentance, and our constant need for Jesus.

Expiation

In expiation, we focus on the cross as the great and only hope for sinners. Here, all songs and readings point to Christ's atoning work. This is also where we observe the Lord's Supper.

Proclamation

Proclamation is the regular, expository preaching of Scripture that seeks to convict and encourage listeners by showing both the law and the gospel in all of Scripture.

Supplication

After the message, one of the elders leads the congregation in prayer in light of the passage preached and the emphasis of the sermon.

Dedication

After a time of prayer, we return to singing in response to the truth of God, committing ourselves to Him and His ways.

Commission

The conclusion of corporate worship is the commission, a sending out of the people into the world by way of a benediction. A benediction is a prayer for God's blessing upon His people. Perhaps the most famous benediction used today is from the book of Numbers:

> *The LORD bless you and keep you;*
> *the LORD make his face to shine upon you and*
>   *be gracious to you;*
> *the LORD lift up his countenance upon you and*
>   *give you peace.*
>
> (NUM. 6:24–26)

The pulpit is the most important gathering in the life of the church, the most critical moment of the week for Christians. Here God's people are gathered together as one, worship the Lord, and feast on His immeasurable grace. A strong liturgy that leads people to see the truth of God and His work, our fallen condition, and our restoration by grace does not create a formal and stiff worship, but a joyfully directed people.

PART 3

the SQUARE

The square in our paradigm represents the public square, the larger environment in which the church has been established. If the table is the church gathered in smaller bands for gospel-based community, and if the pulpit is the church assembled weekly to worship our triune God as one people redeemed by the Son of God and animated by the Spirit of God, then the square is the church sent into the world as salt and light.

> You are the salt of the earth, but if salt has lost its taste, how shall its saltiness be restored? It is no longer good for anything except to be thrown out and trampled under people's feet.

You are the light of the world. A city set on a hill cannot be hidden. Nor do people light a lamp and put it under a basket, but on a stand, and it gives light to all in the house. In the same way, let your light shine before others, so that they may see your good works and give glory to your Father who is in heaven.

(MATT. 5:13–16)

Jesus said that the church is the salt of the earth and the light of the world—easily identifiable and value-adding in their environment. Our saltiness and brightness are seen in our good works in the world. If these qualities are not true of the church, then the church has become useless.

Chapter 8

THE CHURCH IN THE WORLD

Too often, the church is thought of as an isolated entity, the "frozen chosen" that functions more like a holy huddle than a city on a hill whose light shines before the world in a way that unbelievers are won over by our words and works of grace. The church was never intended to be a retreat for the redeemed, but rather a missionary movement that walks boldly in the world to which it has been sent.

In John 20:21, Jesus tells us that He has sent the church into the world just as He was sent by our heavenly Father. How was Jesus sent? As the bearer of good news to a needy people who demonstrated righteousness in all His works and preached life to the perishing. Jesus was sent as a man to live among humanity. And as much as He identified with us, He remained distinct from us, not only as God in flesh, but also as a perfect human.

The church is sent into the world in a similar way: to be a people who demonstrate words and works of grace, obeying our Lord, blessing our neighbors, and preaching the gospel. But we come to the world, in many ways, as one of "them."

Yes, we Christians are made saints by God's grace the moment we believe in Jesus, and this sets us apart from the world. The moment we are born again by the power of the Holy Spirit, our hearts are changed, and we begin to hate much of what the world loves and love much of what the world hates. It is true: we are not of this world, and we cannot align ourselves with the philosophy of the world; but we are also part of the world in a few important ways.

First, we, like all human beings, are made in the image of God. This is a unifying truth for all people. This means that no one person is worth more than another. We stand as equals on level ground as God's image bearers. This means that all people everywhere have incredible value and dignity by virtue of being created in God's image.

Second, we, like all human beings, are sinful. This too is a unifying truth, but it is sad news. All of us have rebelled against God, broken His laws, worshiped false gods, and are therefore worthy of condemnation. This means that all people everywhere are worthy of God's judgment and are in desperate need of His rescue.

Third, we are like our neighbors in that we live in a world marked and marred by sin, and each of us bears the shared responsibility of loving and caring for our neighbors. What the old hymn says is true: "This world is not my home."[1] But what another old hymn says is also true: "This is my Father's world."[2] We all are in this world together.

So when we walk in this world as Christians, we identify with our communities in many ways: as humans created in God's image, marred by sin, and in need of redemption. We are not sent into the world as saviors; for there is only One who saves. Rather, we are sent as His representatives who continue His words and works of mercy.

To say that the church is a people sent means that the entire church must see itself, collectively, as the mission of God entrusted with bringing the good news of salvation to all who will hear us.

What does this mean for a local church? How are we to be in this world?

In principle, this means we must be present, engaged, and known. The local church must live in such a way that the world around it knows it exists. This is more than good signage, advertising campaigns, and mass mailers. It requires the church, as a whole, to be united in its vision and mission, to share the same passion, and to work together toward the same goals. If the glory of God and the gospel of grace are what drive the members of a church, and the mission of the church is shared by all, then a local church will be present, engaged, and known for clear doctrine and good works. The world may embrace some of what we do, but it also will reject much of what we teach. We should not expect anything otherwise, for this is how the world treated our Lord.

Our presence in the world does not mean that we are engaged only in urban areas. The world we are sent into as local churches looks different in every location. Urban, suburban, rural, metropolitan, micropolitan, assisted-living environments, and more are all part of the world we must be engaging as the people of God.

The church will be ineffective and unfruitful if it does not embrace its place in the world. How a church is present and presents itself can and will vary from congregation to congregation. But there are four levels of the public square at which every church should be engaged: participation, restoration, conversation, and multiplication. To those we now turn.

Chapter 9

PARTICIPATION

This first way of engaging the world is the easiest. Simply participate in the culture, as appropriate, however you can. A church's participation in the surrounding community is essential to making inroads to the larger culture and to building bridges with the people in their area. This can be done both as individuals and as an institution (the church formally). Wherever church members can honor God and embrace the community, it is in a position to speak to the people they live among. They are called to represent Christ in every area of life, from vocation to recreation, and this can be accomplished in different ways depending on the surrounding culture and context.

SEASONALLY

Many of us can engage our communities by attending seasonal events. Perhaps there are annual festivals in the summer, autumn, or winter that invite not only onlookers, but also participants in various activities. My city holds scarecrow competitions in the autumn in which many local businesses and organizations compete for fun while sharing with others what they are doing in and for the city. These sorts of events provide incredible opportunities to get to know others in your area.

SOCIALLY

The social aspect of Christian presence in the community is simple, yet most of us do not see it as fundamental to our calling to be salt and light in the world. A Christian who participates in the community intentionally with the goal of following Christ will be conscientious in their patronage.

I encourage the members of Redeemer Fellowship to eat and shop as locally as possible, not only to support local businesses, but also to effect change in town by simply being present where God has placed them. You can be confident that wherever you are, you are there by the will of God. So be present. Be a regular at your favorite spots and get to know those who work there as well as other regulars. When receiving service, tip graciously. Do not fall into the trap of shorting someone because they did not meet your expectations. Instead, show them grace by giving them a tip they do not deserve.

Do not just take up space where you are, but contribute more than you take. Be kind and helpful rather than demanding. This may sound like little more than polite moralism, but it is a small yet important part of following Christ where you live. Take advantage of opportunities to extend the grace and generosity of Christ even in seemingly small ways.

RECREATIONALLY

Sharing hobbies and interests with others in your community creates excellent opportunities to connect with your neighbors and participate in the culture at a healthy level. This affords the opportunity to learn from others and to build friendships that can, in time, provide a context in which long-lasting gospel conversations and counseling can take place naturally.

Running clubs, bowling or softball leagues, reading groups, fantasy football leagues, the local gym, and gaming competitions—these are just a few examples of recreational activities that give Christians and the local church opportunities to live among the people to whom they are called to minister.

But how can churches, and not just individuals, participate at this level? Churches may decide to invest in an aspect of popular recreation by sending teams of people to support such events. For example, at long-distance running events, volunteers are needed to operate water stations and cheering stations along the course. The church may choose to sponsor a recreational or social event aimed at raising awareness of a good cause or real need in the community.

VOCATIONALLY

That some Christians leave their faith and mission in the car before walking into their place of work is not only a missed opportunity to be fully present where God has placed them, but also is a fundamental misunderstanding of the nature of their calling as Christians. One's vocation is their calling to serve the Lord in all of life, and one's employment typically takes up a large portion of their day for five to six days per week. Your job may resonate with the deepest longings of your heart, or it may be tiresome, causing you to long for something better. In either case, where we work is where God has placed us to honor Him and serve others. The apostle Paul said, "Let each person lead the life that the Lord has assigned to him, and to which God has called him. This is my rule in all the churches" (1 Cor. 7:17). Your job is part of what God has assigned you. While you are there, you are called to love and serve others.

This does not mean that Christians should be distributing tracts at every lunch break or that they must start workplace Bible studies before opening hours. But it certainly means that Christians work the same jobs as non-Christians and with non-Christians, but from a completely different point of view and for entirely different purposes. Our work—whether crunching numbers in a cubicle, working construction, answering phones, investing another's money, or teaching elementary school—is not secular work for a Christian. It is sacred. For whatever we do and wherever we work, we do so in the name of Jesus and for the glory of God (Col. 3:17; 1 Cor. 10:30).

Your job is one of the "good works" God has prepared beforehand for you to be faithful in (see Eph. 2:10). Arriving on time, working hard, being honest, showing respect to your employer, and helping your coworkers is not worldly work for the believer, but holy work in and for Jesus Christ.

Chapter 10

RESTORATION

The work of restoration, the next level of engaging the culture, is more difficult than participation because it shifts interest away from the self to the needs of others. By *restoration* I mean the intentional effort to meet the needs of others in such a way that they experience a kind of help, or renewal, even if temporal. It helps people transition out of trouble or need and into a place of safety or satisfaction. Historically, Christians have called this type of ministry "works of mercy."

Puritan Robert Bolton wrote a helpful book on practical Christian living called *General Directions for a Comfortable Walking with God.* Elaborating on works of mercy, he explains that they

> spring from a compassionate heart and fellow feeling,
> affectionately yearning over the temporal wants and
> necessities of our brethren, whereby we are stirred
> up, as occasion is offered, according to our ability,

to succor and support their outward extremities and
distresses; to feed the hungry, to give drink to the
thirsty; to clothe the naked; to entertain the stranger;
to visit the sick; to go to those that are in prison...to
give a helping hand for raising our brethren fallen into
decay (Lev. 25:35), to lend, hoping for nothing again
(Lk. 6:35).[1]

And lest anyone think Bolton believed in helping
only those within the church, he explains we must also
meet the needs of the poor and suffering *in general*—
even the wicked! Bolton wrote that we must work for
the good of all, regardless "whatsoever the party hath
been before; for there thou relievest not his notorious-
ness, but his nature."[2] Our works serve the good of humanity overall.

The work of restoration is a necessary compliment
to the work of proclamation. Anyone who pits words
against works is mistaken. Words and works are brothers that labor together toward the same goal. They have
the same message, and both exist to announce the kingdom of God. As I see it, our proclamation is not full
unless it is done in both word and deed. The deeds are
not simply the pretext for broadcasting a clearer message; they are an inherent part of the message itself. Our
words announce a kingdom; our deeds demonstrate
its presence and our citizenship in it. The question ev-

ery church ought to ask itself is: what work needs to be done in our community to announce that the kingdom has come?

At our church, we offer English as a Second Language classes, a ministry that supplies clothes to the disadvantaged, and a ministry geared toward discipling men in prison. Whether a local church creates new ministries to meet real needs or joins with existing services in their area, the work of restoration takes the shade off of the lamp of the church, allowing its light to shine brightly.

Such work in the community is not the primary work of the church, but a complement to its main work of making disciples and the by-product of being disciples. This means that much of the work of restoration should be done by individuals within the church apart from church-organized activities.

The members of a small group may decide where they will serve the good of the city in tangible ways. A family may dedicate themselves to helping a struggling family or individual in their neighborhood. This is where our work for the good of our city, town, village, or neighborhood reflects and fulfills Jesus' commands to love others.

Look around your city, suburb, neighborhood, or county. What sort of help do your neighbors need? Do you know a widower who lives alone, isolated from others, who needs assistance and friendship? Perhaps you see at-risk youth in need of mentoring. Assisted-living communities and nursing homes are often places where the elderly are segregated from the rest of the community and would be well-served by visitation and real relationships from believers who want nothing in return. Volunteering at a homeless shelter or with clean-up services for local parks, and even getting involved with the town meetings where local issues are being addressed and worked out all provide opportunities to do the hard and fruitful work of mercy.

Restoration happens only when the Great Commandment (Matt. 22:36–40), which calls us to love God and our neighbors, resonates in the hearts of a people rescued by God's grace. Love is one of the most important markers of being present in the world, because most of the time we are engaging not simply ideas, but people—people made in God's image, people who feel, people in need, people Christ calls us to love and serve. It is inappropriate to claim we love our neighbors if we do not demonstrate such love. In all the ways we may be present, it is love for God and others that will move us to speak and act.

Restoration, while meeting immediate needs in your local context, also points to the restoration and renewal of all things that will occur when Jesus returns to vanquish evil, establish peace, reign in justice, and complete our redemption.

As important as the work of restoration is, our focus should not be on the work itself, but on the people in need. And such people need not just *works* of mercy; they need *words* of mercy even more.

Chapter 11

CONVERSATION

More fruitful opportunities are found when we move from restoration to conversation, because, in my experience, most Christians find starting meaningful conversations with others to be more difficult than lending them a helping hand. It is one thing to ladle soup into a bowl or to rake someone's leaves, and quite another to take the time to look into someone's eyes, listen to them, and share the good news with them.

By *conversation*, I mean the exchange of words and ideas with others at every level of human experience. Conversation happens when a Christian speaks with a stranger in the coffee shop, as well as when he or she goes out to the park to evangelize to the lost.

THE IMPORTANCE OF WORDS

Most Christians understand the importance of words. God chose to use written words as the primary way of communicating with us. Our words in ministry are important because they not only comfort, counsel, and correct, but also communicate the heart of our message more quickly and more accurately than our works ever can. In fact, works alone cannot bridge the gap between unbelief and faith. Words must be used because by them God brings people to a saving knowledge of Jesus Christ (Rom. 10:14–15).

Just as we step into the public square carrying out works of mercy, so we must also carry with us words of grace. Words of grace means preaching. Many think of gospel preaching as speaking done from a pulpit, on the street with a megaphone, in confrontational evangelism, in tract distribution, or in door-to-door "visitations." While some of these are valuable and biblical, much of our conversations with non-Christians will take place more plainly and naturally. And when the gospel is offered, there it is still called preaching Christ. A healthy church and her members will talk with others relationally and opportunistically about God and the gospel.

Many love the old line, "Preach the gospel. If necessary, use words." This is falsely attributed to Francis of Assisi, a thirteenth century Roman Catholic preacher. There is no evidence he ever said this, and it is doubtful he would have. The truth is the gospel cannot be preached apart from words. No one will come to faith in Jesus Christ by merely watching the conduct of a Christian or benefitting from the service ministries of a church. The good news of Jesus' life, death, and resurrection for sinners must be heralded, and people must be called to repent of their sin and believe in Christ. They cannot believe if there is nothing to hear: "So faith comes from hearing, and hearing through the word of Christ" (Rom. 10:17).

THE IMPORTANCE OF METHOD

Unfortunately, many Christians are encouraged to talk with non-Christians about Jesus only with the use of a script. Tracts with "Four Spiritual Laws" or "Steps to Peace with God" are common tools used by many to share the gospel. Similar approaches ask diagnostic questions of an individual to get the conversation started: "If you were to die today and stand before God, how would you answer Him if He asked you, 'Why should I let you into heaven?'" These partially or completely scripted conversations can feel unnatural to outsiders. They sense a sales-pitch. They might feel like a target or project instead of a person. Such forced conversations can be used of God, but in my experience, the vast majority of non-Christians find them uncomfortable. It's not the truth as much as the presentation that creates a barrier.

Outsiders know when we are using a script, not because they have heard it before, but because they have had to listen to sales pitches and cold calls throughout their adult lives. We need local churches and church members who are working at being good conversationalists, who are comfortable enough with the truth of the gospel that they can talk through it and its application to others without the aid of a cheat sheet. Only as we learn the art of conversation can we step into the environment of the public square ready to listen to and speak with the people to whom God has sent us.

Conversation requires the church to speak the language of the culture. For most this is easier than they imagine. You probably understand the language of your community, but you may not readily speak it—particularly when it comes to explaining the gospel to people. It is not enough to say the murder of the innocent is an abomination, or that all people are dead in sin and need to be regenerated and justified. We must explain ourselves—even better, the gospel—in words others can understand. Many of us need to learn to rely less on talking points and canned presentations that do not connect with our post-Christian culture, and begin to develop earnest, dialogical methods of engaging others. There's no easy how-to for this beyond simply doing it, failing, and trying again.

Conversation happens not only at the individual level, but also at the institutional level. The church can host open dialogues with non-Christians in the community. Our church holds a monthly Pub Talk that covers topics that are interesting to the people of our city and of eternal value. Various perspectives are represented and shared at these gathering, as it is an open discussion. But as it is sponsored by a church and led by a church member, the truth of Scripture is always supplied in a clear and winsome manner. One of our church plants holds similar public conversations using social media to invite outsiders to a discussion that intersects with faith and theology. His meetings are marked by a large number of atheists, Muslims, skeptics, and New Age adherents.

The work of conversation requires you to be a theologian. Any conversation can quickly turn to things eternal, and many issues regularly brought up are directly related to theological truth. This does not mean that every Christian needs to be as knowledgeable as Augustine, John Owen, or Jonathan Edwards. And I am not suggesting that God cannot overcome our theological inadequacies. But to speak to the culture about good and evil, life and death, why people suffer, sin, the gospel, and the character of God requires us to understand these things well enough to share them—and in an accessible manner. Theological development happens as we read, study, and discuss Scripture with other believers. We mature doctrinally as we learn from good theologians—living and dead, online, at conferences, in books, and in the local church.

Most people in your city are open to a conversation, but are opposed to a lecture. To be heard and understood is valued by all. When we can understand the people in our city, the better equipped we are to rightly apply Scripture to their lives while pointing them to Jesus.

Chapter 12

MULTIPLICATION

The healthy local church's presence in the community should always aim at multiplication, a replication of church health in other churches, both locally and globally. This means that a church's interests must extend beyond its own people, programs, and budget. The two primary ways in which churches can do the work of multiplication is through church planting and church revitalization.

CHURCH PLANTING

Church planting has become a wildly popular approach to ministry in North America. Yet some churches are planted without a calling, without planning, and with mixed motives that can doom a church plant before it even begins. However, I believe that the increased interest in and efforts given to planting new churches in North America is largely good.

Church planting is the establishing of new churches in a given city or region. While no explicit command to start new churches exists in Scripture, the New Testament implies that healthy churches multiply in this sort of manner. The apostle Paul's ministry was characterized by the planting of churches on his mission trips (Rom. 15:19–20; Titus 1:5), and the Great Commission implies the need for churches to be planted as we go throughout the world making and baptizing disciples (Matt. 28:18–20).

The willingness of one church to give of itself for the good of another church requires a kingdom mindset and a desire to reach as many people as possible with the gospel. Such a church is not concerned with building a name for itself or its own brand and is instead captivated by the church universal that Jesus Himself is building.

The work of church planting seems daunting to most churches, especially for those who have never experienced it. How can a church engage in this critical work? There are three basic ways churches participate in the larger work of planting new churches.

Promotion

The easiest step toward involvement in church planting is to get to know solid church planters and church plants, and to help promote them. A church can pray for a church plant regularly during its corporate worship. It is helpful to invite church planters to come and preach at your church. Consider inviting those who will not only proclaim God's Word, but also share what God is doing in their new work. A local church can also send people who are looking for a church to the new church in their area. By building relationships with church plants, you will find yourself in a better position to get involved.

Partnering

Another way to get involved in church planting is to put your money—or your people—where your mouth is. You can participate in church planting through financial support, encouraging your church members to join a plant, and to offer help as an established church. Church planters need coaching, and local church leadership has experience that could prove helpful to planters. Your church might not send a planter, but it can partner with a sending church in a variety of ways.

Planting

Many churches could plant a church in the next few years if they really wanted to. If a church is seeking out and raising up future leaders in their congregation, they may find themselves with good men called to lead a plant. If you find yourself with qualified men, or even men with potential and a sense of calling, you will need help in this process. Help abounds in networks like Acts 29 and denominations like the Southern Baptist Convention. They have resources, assessment processes, coaching, and even financial support in some cases that help churches send out planters.

We need more partnerships between churches and we need more churches. Working together to plant churches is a biblical way to fulfill the Great Commission to make disciples.

CHURCH REVITALIZATION

An often neglected aspect of multiplication is revitalization. Every church has a life-cycle. It is planted, it grows, it bears much fruit, and in time it may wither and even die. As many of the churches in our cities have slowly stopped reaching people and experience decline, they are nearing the end. Rather than leave these churches to fend for themselves, healthier churches should seek opportunities to assist them so they may be revitalized.

A revitalized church is one that will cultivate and maintain all three environments. The table will be a thriving environment of fellowship, friendship, and mutual edification. Hospitality will begin to mark the community of faith. Scripture and prayer will be shared outside of the Sunday gathering as believers come together.

The pulpit will return to a Word-driven, theologically grounded, God-centered worship service where the people are eager to gather in order to draw near to God the way He has prescribed and to experience His convicting, encouraging, and transforming work in their lives together.

The square will no longer be a place to hide from, ignore, or resent, but will be seen as the very place God has sent the church to reach as many as possible with the gospel.

Often, churches in decline do not have a pastor and would benefit from another church supplying them with regular preachers. Other churches need help in solving deep-seated problems to which they are too close to even see. Many churches simply need counsel on how to unite a congregation around a common vision and mission. From simply befriending other local churches that are struggling to offering coaching, there are multiple ways that healthy churches can serve struggling churches around them.

Part of what makes multiplication possible is cooperation. The mission Jesus gave the church is carried out better through denominations, conventions, associations, networks, and even informal fellowships of local churches than through local churches working on their own. Shared theology and resources make for great partnerships in reaching the lost and making disciples. Most of the healthy and growing churches in our cities cooperate with a number of other churches. They do not believe they can fulfill Christ's commission on their own, because they know they are not supposed to work alone. The church's work of multiplication occurs at both local and global levels. We are to take seriously Jesus' call to be His witnesses even to the uttermost parts of the earth. Churches, therefore, are commissioned to look not only beyond the four walls of their buildings, but also beyond their countries and continents. Multiplication orients the local church to the global mission of God.

Working out our salvation in the public square demands great personal conviction. Like Jesus and the apostles, preaching the gospel in word and deed will both lead to you being favored as a helper, and hated as a meddler. It just depends on the issue. Everyone who labors in such work will encounter fear. Comfort and courage will only come from God who has promised that we are blessed when persecuted, and that the gates of hell will not prevail against His church.

CONCLUSION

The life of the church is experienced in three environments: the table, pulpit, and square. These are the distinct contexts in which we evangelize and make disciples, and they help us answer the question: what does a church do? The answer is we follow Christ and make disciples in these three environments. Until we see how the local church can be faithful to the Lord in these three environments, we will struggle to fulfill Christ's call. The more organized and focused a church is in these three environments, the more fruitful, steady, and healthy it becomes.

The environment of the table brings church members together for mutual edification and fellowship, which leads to lasting friendships in which believers can carry out the commands to love, serve, encourage, rebuke, and help one another. Without this environment, we cannot function relationally as the church. Most of the commands God gives us can in fact be carried out only in this context.

The environment of the pulpit serves as the central environment of the church, not because most of our time is spent there—it is not—but because the pulpit interprets the whole of our lives and helps us see the truth of God who reigns in all three environments. Here the church worships our triune God in spirit and truth, and its members are bound together by a shared faith and common confession. If the church neglects this environment, we cannot be the church Christ calls us to be.

The square is the particular environment the church is sent into: the local public square where our words and works of grace point those who are perishing to the Savior who rescues. Without this environment, we will struggle not only to engage the culture, but also to reach people with the good news of God's love for sinners and the hope we have in Jesus Christ.

A healthy church will live in all three environments intentionally, strategically, and passionately.

NOTES

Chapter 2: Smaller Groups

1. Joanne Jung, *Godly Conversation: Rediscovering the Puritan Practice of Conference* (Grand Rapids: Reformation Heritage Books, 2011). Kindle Edition.
2. Ibid., Kindle Locations 2010–2011.
3. Ibid., Kindle Locations 2157–2159.
4. "Heidelberg Catechism," Q&A 55, Reformed Church of America website, https://www.rca.org/resources/heidelbergcatechism.

Part 2: The Pulpit

1. Edmund P. Clowney, "Corporate Worship: A Means of Grace" in *Give Praise to God: A Vision for Reforming Worship*, eds. Philip Graham Ryken, Derek W. H. Thomas, J. Ligon Duncan III (Downers Grove, IL: InterVarsity Press, 1995), 95.

Chapter 5: The Word in Worship

1. "The Baptist Confession of Faith," 22.1, on *The Voice of the Reformation* website, http://www.vor.org/truth/1689/1689bc00.html.
2. Ibid., 1.6.

Chapter 6: Worshiping in Spirit and Truth

1. Henry Scudder, *The Christian's Daily Walk*, (Hinton, VA: Sprinkle Publication, 1998), 130.

2. Richard Steele, *A Remedy for Wandering Thoughts in Worship* (Hinton, VA: Sprinkle Publication, 1998), 243.

3. Ibid.

4. Ibid., 244.

5. Scudder, 236.

Chapter 8: The Church in the World

1. Albert E. Brumley, "This World Is Not My Home," on *Songs & Hymns of Revival* website, http://hymnal.calvarybaptistsv .org/485.html.

2. Maltbie Davenport Babcock, "This Is My Father's World," on *The Cyber Hymnal* website, http://www.cyberhymnal.org/htm/t/i/ tismyfw.htm.

Chapter 10: Restoration

1. Robert Bolton, *General Directions for a Comfortable Walking with God* (Morgan, PA: Soli Deo Gloria Publications, 1991), 283–284.

2. Ibid., 284.

ACKNOWLEDGMENTS

I would like to thank Paul Maxwell for encouraging me to write this book and introducing me to Moody Publishers. Thanks to Drew Dyck, acquisitions editor, and Kevin Emmert, developmental editor, for helping me clarify and better communicate what is on my heart. This book is greatly improved by your efforts.

Thanks to the leadership of Redeemer Fellowship— Jeff Willey, Pat Aldridge, Brian Malcolm, Rob Warford, and Jimmy Fowler—and the entire congregation for showing me what a healthy church looks like in real life.

And thank you to my wife, Jen, and our children, Katherine, Elias, Madeline, and Kilian, for being patient with me during the time it took to write this book.

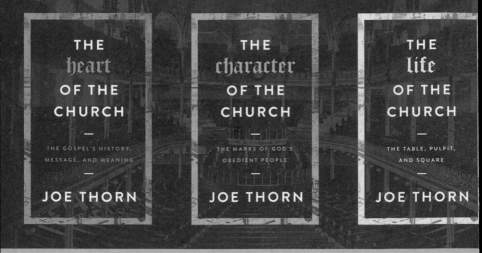

THE **life** | **heart** | **character** OF THE CHURCH

This three-book series is designed for diverse readership. It avoids theological jargon and uses clear terms to keep readers tracking and engaged. Ideal for evangelism and discipleship, each book can be read within an hour and is organized simply for retention. Biblical, balanced, and historically informed, it is useful for Sunday school, one-to-one reading, ministry training, and personal study.

FOR THE
CHURCH

FTC.CO

MOODY
Publishers®

moodypublishers.com

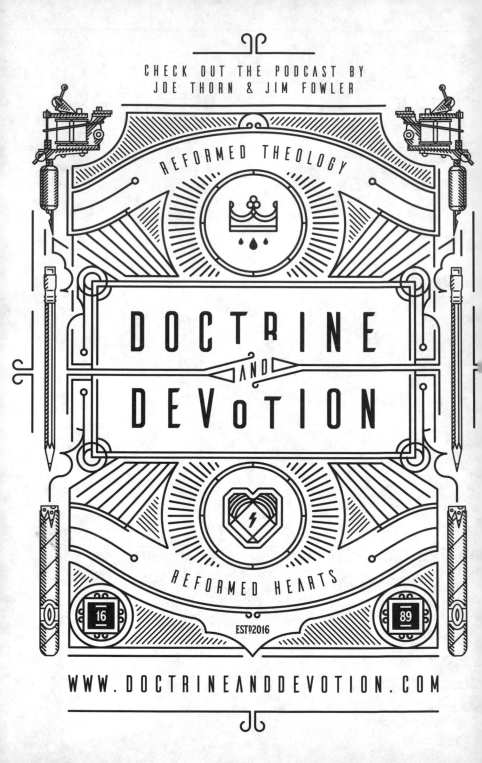